Quick Web

A Beginner's Guide To Selling Your Stuff On Craigslist

STEVE BUELOW

New Media Jet, LLC
United States of America

Cover layout and design New Media Jet, LLC.
Published in the United States of America
by New Media Jet, LLC.

Visit us online at NewMediaJet.com.

ISBN: 978-0615811307

*Dedicated to the friends you'll meet
and the stuff you'll sell...*

Contents
A Beginner's Guide...

What Do I Do With All This Stuff?

"Everyone lives by selling something."
– Robert Louis Stevenson

It's a question countless people ask every day, and in the next hour or so you will learn how to connect with buyers that are sincerely eager to purchase:

All of that stuff that's just gathering dust and cluttering your closets, your basement or garage, and that spare room that you've been dreaming about using for the last several years.

But first, I want to take just a moment to say thanks. Thank you for purchasing your copy of *Quick Web Sales: A Beginner's Guide To Selling Your Stuff On Craigslist.*

Thank you!

Your timing couldn't be better. You see, right this minute, as you are reading these words, thousands of transactions – no, likely tens of thousands of transactions – are being finalized online and over the telephone by average, everyday people just like you and me.

Buyer and seller brought together online in a virtual market, engaged in one of the oldest dances in business.

You have something of value (a product) that I'd like to own. At the same time, I also have something of value (my hard-earned money) that you'd like to own!

It's a thing of beauty.

And, thankfully, today's online market offers us many advantages over the past methods such as running endless ads in the local newspaper or parting with our possessions for peanuts in a rummage sale or garage sale after expending a significant amount of time, energy, and expense.

Recently, while speaking with someone who was preparing for an upcoming garage sale, I made the mistake of commenting something along the lines of "That sounds like fun!"

Wow... was I unprepared for
what happened next!

My friend was definitely not excited about the prospects. You see, she's already more than busy and has her plate more than full as a single mom:

➢ Working a full-time job
➢ Volunteering with children's school activities
➢ Taking care of her home
➢ Shopping and paying her bills
➢ Watching over her aging parents

And now she's about to
spend three entire evenings...

...organizing and labeling, then taking a vacation day on Friday, only to sit in a chair in her driveway for the next two days as countless strangers haggle relentlessly in an attempt to further devalue her possessions, and whittle to the bare bones items that were already priced at just pennies on the dollar to begin with!

Worse, at the end of the sale, anything that isn't sold has to be packed up and hauled away or sent back to clutter up the spare room that she was trying to clean out in the first place!

Hmm... I asked how much she made at her last sale. After paying the babysitter, adding in the cost of all her advertising and the refreshments that she provided for her sister and the neighbors she recruited to help her, she cleared just under $270. Yikes.

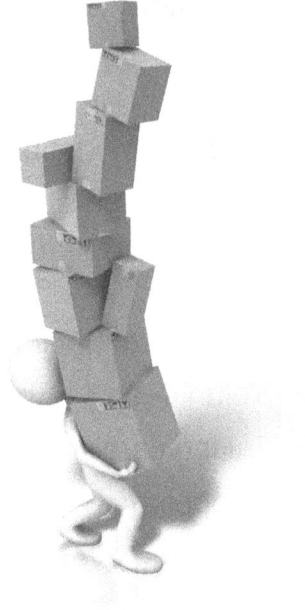

There's a better way!

A moment ago, I referenced the interaction that goes on between buyers and sellers in general, especially in private-party person-to-person transactions. Each party is interested in the transfer of property or ownership from one person to another.

That's simple enough. But beyond that, the goals are absolutely and completely opposing:

**You, as the seller, want to complete the sale
at the highest possible price.**

After all, it is your merchandise, you typically have memories attached, and you did all of the work in preparing it for sale in the first place.

**On the other hand, the buyer wants to make
the purchase as cheaply as humanly possible.**

He or she typically has no emotional attachment, often presents an attitude that seems unfriendly or uncaring, and appears to be ready to walk away at a moment's notice if they don't get their way.

In the past, this was a game where the advantage clearly went to the buyer, leaving sellers like you and me wondering whether we were completely wasting our time, often feeling frustrated, rejected, or disappointed with our results, and anxious just to get the whole thing over with. If you've ever spent an entire week of your life in the rummage sale process... you know what I mean.

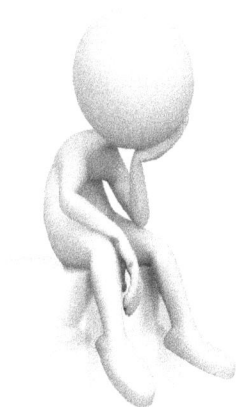

This book is for the seller!
More importantly...

- ➢ If the previous story resonates with you
- ➢ If you know you have items of value
- ➢ If as a rule you take good care of your things
- ➢ If you are interested in a relaxing process that will bring honest and willing buyers to your home, eager to pay a fair price for your well-loved and gently-used possessions

...then, this book is for you!

It is critical to understand the sincerity of that last statement. I did not write *Quick Web Sales: A Beginner's Guide To Selling Your Stuff On Craigslist* for everyone. I wrote it for you.

What I'm going to say next is an important distinction in a world where online marketers seem to be hawking get-rich-quick schemes in every digital corner. Here's what this book *will not* teach you!

This book will not teach you to buy and sell foreclosed properties on Craigslist... or travel the world, earning five-figures a month as you support yourself and your extended relatives through the online merchandising of everything from pirates' plunder and buried treasure to questionable international commodities deals. It won't suggest that you borrow from your home equity to purchase entire lots on the auction block to resell online... and it won't promise to allow you to retire as a Craigslist millionaire in the next 2-5 years.

In case you're wondering, yes, those ideas and schemes are actually out there, and like all products in a free enterprise system, I suppose they're produced to fill some need within various niches in society. While I am certainly no one's judge, I want to make it clear that *this book is not written* for any of those markets.

On the contrary, *Quick Web Sales: A Beginner's Guide To Selling Your Stuff On Craigslist* was written particularly to help those with limited online, sales or marketing experience – *beginners* – to get up and running in minutes with time-tested and successful selling principles that work really well on Craigslist.

So, if you are one of the 99.7% of potential users who are squeezed for cash and could use some extra money this week, someone who has valuable items that you're not currently or recently using, and you'd like to sell them in exchange for a reasonable amount of money in a win-win transaction, then this book is absolutely for you.

It is my desire to see you take hold of the new technology and tools that allow you to connect and sell your items today.

As you turn these pages, you will learn to:

- Sell items you're not using and get cash fast
- Create eager buyers and even repeat buyers
- Discover the best times to post your ads
- Write headlines and copy that get attention now
- Use search terms to get your ads found
- Easily separate yourself from your competition
- Avoid scam artists and ripoffs
- Develop confidence in yourself and the process
- Determine fair prices and eliminate negotiating

Want more?

Okay, you'll also:

➢ Find a wealth of safety and privacy tips
➢ Learn to avoid common and costly mistakes
➢ Receive *EXACT STRATEGIES* and also *ACTUAL ADS* that I have used to generate thousands of dollars in as little as just a few short weeks!

So what are we waiting for?

Let's get started!

Chapter One

Selling On Craigslist: The Basics

"Who in the world is Craig, and what is his list?"
– Me, the first time I heard of Craigslist

If you're like most people, you've probably heard of Craigslist, or specifically the website located at:

www.craigslist.org

In fact, since you're here, I'm almost sure you're familiar with it, or you wouldn't be reading this book!

At the same time, if you're like most people:

> ➢ You've seldom bought anything on Craigslist
> ➢ You've seldom listed anything on Craigslist
> ➢ You've seldom sold anything on Craigslist
> ➢ You don't have an active account on Craigslist
> ➢ It's been so long since you've visited that you can't remember your password on Craigslist!

And as popular as the site is, most people still have many questions surrounding the simple ins and outs of using Craigslist effectively and often, and they certainly don't understand how to turn unused or no longer wanted items into decent cash... *FAST!*

Here's a great question I overheard
my wife ask someone just now:

"Would you rather have...
$2 at a rummage sale this weekend,
or $35 on Craigslist tonight?"

Sounds simple enough... but it really is the choice you have. At this moment, Craigslist may very well be the best option available to you to sell all those items you have lying around – quickly, easily, and at a fair price!

Craigslist began in 1995 in San Francisco, California when founder Craig Newmark acted on an idea he had to help people out by providing free classified advertising on a local level.

Obviously, he hit upon a real need and a desire that people had to connect and come together on any number of shared interests from jobs and apartment rentals to romance, business services, buying and selling used personal merchandise, and much more.

The topic of this book covers one of those aspects – the opportunity that you have to sell your stuff and get some cash as quickly as the next few hours – and it answers the basic question of every beginner:

"Just how do I get started selling my stuff on Craigslist?"

Now, please understand that if you are asking that question today, **you are not alone.** In fact, even among those who have listed items frequently, *actually selling them* can be a whole different matter.

I was speaking with one of our customers recently who had purchased several hundred dollars worth of goods from us over a two week period.

She is a Craigslist buyer.
She is not a Craigslist seller.

…but she would like to be.

Now, contrary to what you might have heard:

➢ Becoming a Craigslist seller is easy
➢ The website is simple to navigate
➢ The search function is excellent
➢ There are LOTS of buyers for your stuff
➢ You can sell at your convenience
➢ You can maintain your privacy
➢ You can get top dollar without negotiating

And you can also clean out your house, have fun, and make a few new friends along the way!

Oh... and did I mention
CASH in your pocket before bedtime?

The secret is to learn and apply some basic principles and strategies regarding your:

➢ Product
➢ Pricing
➢ Competitors
➢ Ad layout
➢ Messaging
➢ Interactions, conversations, and follow-up

In other words, you need a system.

Chapter Two

What Do You Have To Sell?

"In the second part of life you get rid of stuff you've accumulated."
– Mikhail Baryshnikov

I was speaking with a friend earlier today about Craigslist. Well, actually the conversation didn't start out about Craigslist, it began with a discussion about the fact that:

She needs some cash right now!

And not even a lot of cash...

Just forty or fifty bucks before her next paycheck would be really helpful in taking the edge off! And she's not alone. Who couldn't use a few extra $20 bills right now? I could, and likely so could you. And you have some stuff that you can easily sell in the next 24 hours!

Want an example?
Check out this kitchen cart!

Seemed like a great idea when we bought it, but it just wasn't getting used the way we thought it would.

So we had three choices:

1) Let it hang around unused a few more years
2) Try to convince our daughter it is an heirloom
3) Sell it now and make better use of the cash!

SOLD – and for more than I even asked!!

Yes, I thought you'd like that – and don't you worry...

*I'm going to show you exactly how
I create the winning ads that can get
you full price offers and then some!*

This is what my friend found so amazing!

When she was telling me about her need, I asked her what she had lying around that she could sell.

"Oh gosh, Steve, I don't have time to put together a sale," she said. "I've got three tests in the next week and a half, and I'm volunteering at – "

"Why don't you put something up on Craigslist... it's easy," I suggested.

There was a stunned silence... then she offered her own Craigslist story. It seems that in the past, she has – like countless others – thrown together a few ads and put them up on Craigslist... to no avail.

Over a period of time, she has listed a couch, a bedroom set, several tools, some other miscellaneous items, and her kitchen table and chairs. Next, she asked the BIG question:

"Have *you* ever sold anything on Craigslist?"

*Having sold several thousand dollars worth of items
in just the past month or so alone, I had to smile.
I knew I could help her. And I can help you, too!*

As I said, my friend had tried without success to sell
a couch... but we sold our couch. In fact, this couch:

She had tried without success to sell tools... yet
I sold this saw for darn-near as much as I paid for it:

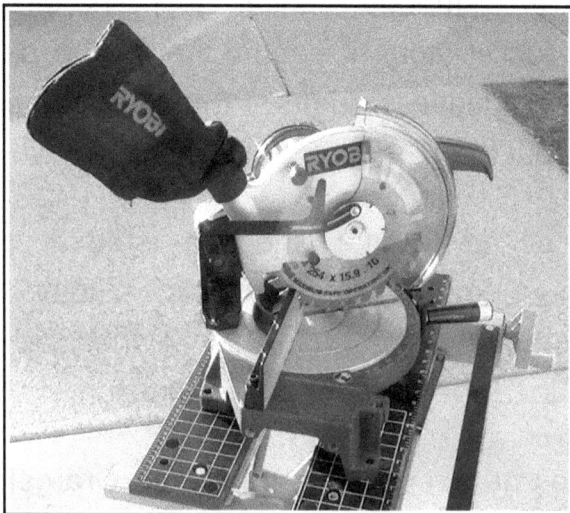

And she had tried without success to sell her kitchen table and chairs... at the very same time that we were selling this beautiful dining set (without negotiating) in less than 24 hours:

So what's the difference? Why is one person able to seemingly list whatever he or she wants and have buyers coming out of the woodwork, while thousands of other people put ads on Craigslist and get nowhere at all?

Quite simply, it's the system.

And that's exactly what I'm going to give you. Regardless of what you are looking to sell, there are people out there who would love to own it. These simple strategies will make the process profitable.

**But first, you'll need to find some stuff to sell...
and getting started can be scary!**

There's a reason all that stuff is hiding in your closets, the basement, the garage and the attic. In fact, over the years, it seems that many homes start to look a lot like mini-storage facilities where pantry shelves, dresser drawers, and cupboards accumulate piles of unused and unwanted items that no longer add value to the owner's life. Why do we do that?

Sometimes we hang onto things because of a past emotional connection. Other times, we believe we might just need the item in the future. Yet, often, we'd be thrilled to sell certain objects if it didn't seem so difficult, time consuming, and...

...if only the price was right.

Start with all those unique tools and gadgets that seemed like such a good idea on the TV infomercials, but that rarely, if ever, get used.

Here are some places around your home you may want to look and some items you may want to consider:

Kitchen:

- extra pots and pans
- dishes and dish racks
- cloths and towels
- appliances, ranges
- refrigerators, freezers
- pizza or toaster ovens
- dehydrators, juicers
- salad spinners
- can openers, blenders
- cooking/serving utensils
- pot holders
- cutting boards
- place mats
- fondue sets
- coffee or tea makers
- ice cream makers
- spice racks
- dutch ovens
- recipe books
- bread makers
- microwave ovens
- popcorn poppers
- coolers, range hoods
- dining tables and chairs
- serving carts, TV trays
- cleaning tools/supplies

Bathroom:

- hair dryers and curlers
- hair cutters and trimmers
- cosmetic mirrors
- towel racks and towels
- cabinets and organizers
- scales and light fixtures

Family and Living Room:

- unwanted furniture
- coffee tables, recliners
- couches/sofas/ottomans
- TV stands, bookshelves
- desks, chairs, end tables
- office equipment
- centerpieces, aquariums
- picture frames, clocks
- candle holders
- video/board games, toys
- exercise equipment
- books, former interests
- previous hobbies
- audio/video tapes
- CD/DVD/video players
- coin collections
- stamp collections
- magazine collections
- ornamental collections
- album collections
- card collections
- sports/other collectibles
- stereo/radio equipment
- televisions, electronics
- cameras, fax machines
- GPS, old cell phones
- old land line phones
- art works, pottery
- musical instruments
- antiques of every kind

Bedrooms, Pantries, and Closets:

- season-specific outfits
- jackets, shoes, boots
- dresses, skirts, blouses
- scarves, belts, gloves
- sweaters, sunglasses
- jeans, hats
- wedding ensembles
- formal/business suits
- maternity clothing
- jewelry/jewelry boxes
- music boxes, rings
- bracelets, necklaces
- broaches, pins
- cuff links, watches
- beds and bedding
- baby cribs/bassinets
- dressers and bureaus
- armoires, garment racks
- sewing machines
- irons and ironing boards
- laundry carts/baskets
- manicure/pedicure sets
- medical stuff, canes
- walkers, crutches
- wheelchairs
- testing equipment
- unused sports stuff
- bowling balls
- rollerblades, scooters
- baseball gloves
- footballs, helmets
- tennis racquets
- flashlights, extra luggage
- vacuums
- steam cleaners
- games and more games

Basement, Garage, Storage Unit and Yard:

- tools, air conditioners
- heaters, dehumidifiers
- gardening and yard stuff
- more tools, bikes/trikes
- wheelbarrows/wagons
- snow blowers/shovels
- lawn mowers, fertilizers
- leaf blowers, weedeaters
- landscaping products
- chainsaws, grills
- car stuff, hobby stuff
- personal watercraft
- boat or RV stuff
- snowmobiles or ATV's
- motorcycle stuff, tires
- wood working materials
- pool cues, yard games
- golf clubs, camping stuff
- washers and dryers
- old computer stuff
- construction/painting stuff
- hunting and fishing gear
- air pumps/compressors
- artificial Christmas trees
- obsolete decorations
- ski/snowboarding stuff
- hoses, wood splitters
- bird feeders and baths
- storage buckets
- containers, ladders, rugs
- patio furniture
- team sports equipment

Chapter Three

Selling For The Highest Price

"Price is what you pay. Value is what you get."
– Warren Buffett

What if I told you that you could set a fair price, have interest from multiple buyers, and then sell your items on Craigslist for what they're really worth – without the sometimes-ugly process of haggling and negotiating?

Well, you can.

I began this book by laying out one of the great imbalances of selling at rummage or garage sales.

Such environments typically attract people who are engaged in impulse buying, meaning that they're not necessarily looking for what you have to sell. Instead, they're just looking for "a deal."

**They're hoping to get something for nothing...
or just next to nothing.**

They also have no emotional connections or memories tied to those personal items that you have emotional connections or memories tied to.

You know, like the:

> ➤ Children's clothing that has been packed away for years
> ➤ Tools you inherited and never used from your grandfather
> ➤ Jewelry from past relationships that you've been hanging onto
> ➤ Souvenirs from past trips that you no longer have room for
> ➤ Duplicate gifts that you received for birthdays or anniversaries
> ➤ Now-aging appliances that you received as wedding gifts that need to be replaced
> ➤ And on and on.

To you, these things are meaningful.

And mine are meaningful to me. It can be difficult enough to part with our possessions without putting them out at some cheap garage sale, and having carload after carload of strangers walk onto our property and tell us our things aren't worth anything!

We don't want people playing negotiating games. We don't want them turning up their noses. And we don't want them offering us a ridiculous price for something of value.

No, if we're going to part with our belongings, we want them to go to someone who will appreciate them as much as we do. And it all begins with the rules we set and the value we establish.

Enter Craigslist.

When selling individual items or even bundled items on Craigslist, in most cases you are connecting with individuals who are in the process of intentionally seeking and searching for a specific item. They have likely viewed similar products or brands online or in a local store and they understand what it would cost to get it brand new. They're not out running from rummage sale to yard

sale to garage sale hoping to bump into the object of their desire out of sheer luck.

On the contrary, they are now on Craigslist, actively searching to find out who might have a quality used alternative for a reasonable cost – for a fair price.

That is what they are seeking.

And never forget, until someone places the cash in your hand, it is your property – you can choose to sell it to whomever you like, whenever you like, wherever you like, and at whatever price you like.

Further, when selling on Craigslist, your initial interaction with a potential buyer will be over the phone, or by text or e-mail. You don't have to give your address, and you won't have a crew of rummage sale people standing in your driveway, picking through your things. You can easily shut down the conversation in the span of a few seconds and choose not to sell it at all if you don't like the way that initial call goes.

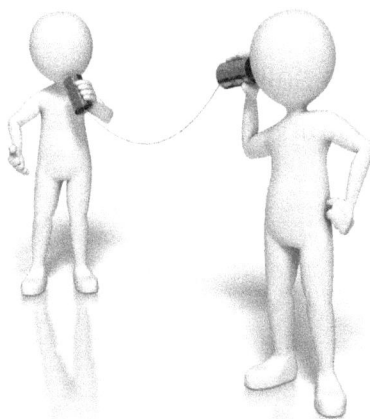

With that in mind, here are a few questions to consider in establishing the resale value of your items:

- *What am I selling?*
- *Why am I selling?*
- *Who is my likely buyer?*
- *What is the benefit to my buyer?*
- *What are the most likely search terms?*
- *Why is this item valuable or useful?*
- *What are its best characteristics?*
- *What is unique about it?*
- *Is it in working order?*
- *Are there cosmetic defects?*
- *If so, can they be quickly & inexpensively repaired?*
- *Is my item as clean as it could be?*
- *Are there components that I can itemize?*
- *Is there anything I can throw in as a bonus?*
- *What did I pay when I bought it new?*
- *What would I pay if I bought it new today?*
- *Does its condition represent its value?*
- *Does my price represent its value?*
- *Who else is selling this item used, and at what price?*

In a moment, I'll give you a real life example of how I used this information to sell an 8-year-old heater that I no longer needed... for nearly 61% of the original purchase price, instead of $10 at a garage sale!

*But first, let me just say that because
of my background in sales and marketing,
I tend to like to track things.*

Here's why:

If I find that an ad is really getting a terrific response, I want to be able to repeat those successful actions. At the same time, if an idea isn't working, it helps to know exactly what I was doing that didn't work!

So the first thing I did was create a little form like the one on the next page, using the questions I felt were most applicable. You don't have to recreate the wheel – just copy mine.

You have my permission!

In the beginning, I found it very helpful to have these types of forms or checklists, and it saved me the trouble of trying to remember what I did last time.

As you work with these ads more and more, it will become second nature to think in terms of your buyer or customer, to phrase things in such a way that not only resonates with that person individually, but also immediately and effectively separates you from everyone else out there who is offering a similar item for sale.

What am I selling?
Portable propane heater (torpedo heater)

Why am I selling?
Moving — no longer have use for it

Who is my likely buyer?
Blue-collar, outdoor sports enthusiast, hobbyist

What is the benefit to my buyer?
Looks and works like new, half the price

What are the most likely search terms?
Propane, heater, torpedo, heat, btu, shop

Why is this item valuable or useful?
Quickly heats uninsulated garage or shop

What are its best characteristics?
Small, light-weight, powerful, economical

What is unique about it?
Best value on Craigslist

Is it in working order?
Perfect, starts on first click... no defects

Is my item as clean as it could be?
Yes, actually shines!

Are there components that I can itemize?
Heater, hose, and regulator

Is there anything I can throw in as a bonus?
Empty propane tank

What is the cost new?
I paid $99 eight years ago... is $109 today

Does my price represent its value?
Absolutely

Other sellers' used price?
$30-60 on Craigslist

Right now...

Let's take the information from the form on the previous page and see how it relates to the ad copy I wrote for the heater I sold.

Then, in chapter five, we'll break down the nine components of this winning ad, and in chapter seven you'll receive the individual strategies that guide the way it was written, the pictures that I used, the phone messages I set up, the interactions that I had with the various callers, and the conversation with the winning buyer.

Remember, the goal is simple and twofold:

1) Grab the attention of your prospective buyer
2) Create a preference for your product

Done well, your ad may stop the buyer's search altogether.

Keep this in mind: most people are working harder today than ever. They're tired, they're often stressed, and they don't want to spend all evening with the little free time they have searching endless ads for used merchandise online and calling sellers they don't know or trust.

**They just want to get the process over with.
Your goal is to help them do just that.**

By the way, to showcase the power of this system, the following ad generated nearly thirty-five ready buyers – cash in hand – several of whom offered to **bid the price up an additional 30%** from what I had set in my Craigslist posting. Had I wanted to go that route, it is likely I could've had a bidding war right up to the $99 price that I paid for it eight years earlier.

Try that at a rummage sale where your items are devalued nearly out of existence! Here's how the pics were laid out on the ad, and I have reprinted the text of the posting on page 41:

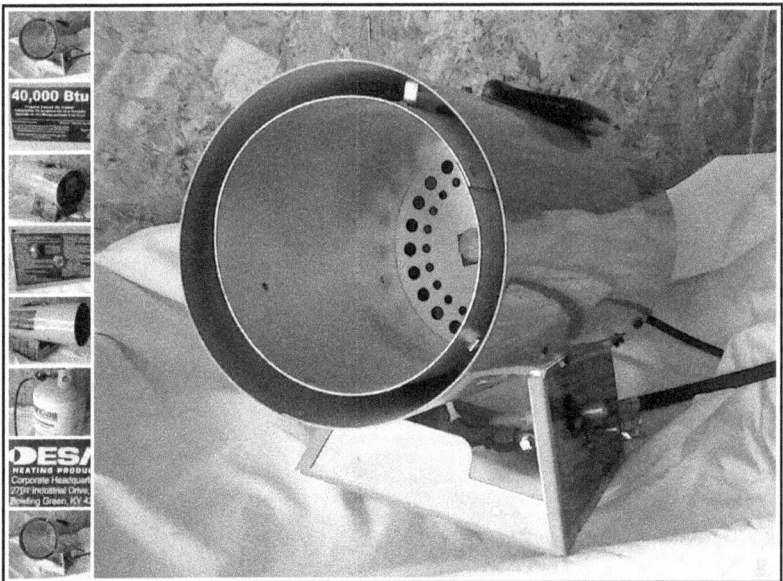

My ad was clean, just like the heater I was selling... with eight total pictures and care taken to make sure that it looked as good as it possibly could.

And as you read the ad on the following page, keep in mind that the closest competing ad for a heater of similar price, size, and output had a single picture of a white, rusted heater standing up on end against a pile of junk in a shed, with one line underneath that read:

"Pretty old but still works – asking $60 obo"

Here's the truth: more often than not, that is what you're competing with on Craigslist. Your competitors have low expectations, and in many cases treat their own possessions like they're not worth anything... and that's exactly what they get.

Now I'll share another very simple truth. Most people who have been conditioned by selling at various rummage or garage sales believe that they must negotiate down to the lowest price in order to move their goods. Notice the "obo," meaning "or best offer."

Don't buy into that.

Here's the ad I wrote that had buyers trying to bid the price *up*. I recommend using it as a model:

The Best Little Torpedo Heater on Craigslist. Location: By Airport

It might be cold outside but it'll be smokin' wherever you are with this little beauty. We moved from a home into a condo-type place and I can't find anything to use it for or I'd definitely keep it for myself. 40,000 btu's will definitely warm your shop or garage or anywhere else you choose to use it!

I bought it brand new for $99 on sale, and as you can see by the pics, I took darn good care of it and it might as well still be brand new today. Oh, and it also includes the hose kit with the regulator (which I paid another $29 for, a total of $128) and you can also have the empty propane tank pictured to use as a trade in so you won't have to pay a deposit on your first one! How long do you think this will last?

Your opportunity to own this awesome heater will be determined by the order in which your call is received. No negotiating necessary... you know it's already a steal at $59. Come and get it.

Thanks for your interest,
Steve
(xxx) xxx-xxxx

**Compare that to the competition's
"Pretty old but still works – asking $60 obo"**

You'll notice from the quick form I filled out back on page 37 that similar items had an asking price of $30-60 on Craigslist. And regarding negotiating, I will also tell you that most of those sellers were likely to be willing to negotiate down and accept an offer of a fraction of their asking price if questioned.

More on that in a minute... now take a look:

First, I did not set an "asking price." On the contrary, I set a "sales price" – the price for which they could make my heater, their heater.

And what did I set as my sales price? $59... exactly one dollar below the highest asking price.

Next, what did I put in the same sentence with the price? I book-ended it right in the middle of these words:

"No negotiating necessary... you know it's already a steal... Come and get it."

And come and get it they did! In fact, the winning buyer – the very first person who called – gave me three crisp $20 bills, and when I said I'd run in the house to get his change, he told me to keep the buck! He also asked me to call him first the next time I am selling any tools or outdoor lawn or sports equipment.

And that, my friend, is how it's done. We'll break down all the other nuances of the ad in chapter five, but right now, let's talk further about the subject of negotiating… or better yet, not negotiating.

Here's what I'd like you to do:

Imagine going into your local grocery store tomorrow, loading up your entire cart, and then proceeding to the checkout like you do every other time you shop. The store employee scans your items (or maybe you do it yourself), and it's time to pay.

Except, this time, I want you to try something different.

Instead of paying the bill, tell the clerk that you will only give them 80% of what they asked – then, put the money down, and proceed to bag your things.

What do you think will happen next?

➤ Will they accept your terms?

➤ Will they make you a counter offer?

➤ Will they call a manager?

➤ Will they call the police?

Try the same at the gas station or the doctor's office or your local bookstore. Sounds ridiculous, doesn't it.

**The truth is that negotiating or haggling
is simply not accepted in many areas
of our economy. In others, it is.**

Of all the industries out there, none is probably more synonymous with the concept of negotiating – or haggling, as it is often called – than the automobile industry and the act of car buying.

Yet, even here, "No Haggle Dealerships" and "No Haggle Pricing" are becoming popular for one major reason: people don't like negotiating.

In fact, I read a survey some time ago that suggested nearly two-thirds of all car buyers would prefer to choose their car and pay one set price...

...if only they could trust the price.

And therein lies the issue.

The reason people think they have to haggle over the price of a car is because they feel it has been artificially inflated to begin with.

They don't believe the asking price is a fair price...
that the asking price is representative
of the value or vice versa.

In that case, there are only two ways to even the scales, and both entail negotiating. Either:

1) Add more options, or
2) Lower the price

But what if the price is already perceived as fair?

➢ What if you, the buyer, already recognized and acknowledged the value in the transaction?
➢ What if the salesperson was making you the same offer that was made to everyone else who bought the same package?
➢ What if the auto dealership did business just like they do at the grocery store?
➢ What if you were excited and already believed you were receiving a good and fair deal?

Then the sale is simple...
and no negotiating is necessary.

That is your job when selling anything. Make the price fair. When I say that I set the sales price and don't negotiate, it is because I have already established a price that I believe to be fair. And once in a while, I'm wrong. I have on a very rare occasion pulled an ad down, edited the price and put it back up again... but I don't negotiate.

When a seller asks for a higher price, all the while knowing they'd gladly accept a lower price, I believe that likely means that they knew it was overpriced to begin with. And I don't do that.

Does that mean I have never had
people who want to negotiate?

No, but it happens very rarely. Even after stating clearly that there's "No negotiating necessary..." there are still going to be some people that just can't help themselves and feel the need to ask something along the lines of, "Hi, I saw your ad says $59... would you take $50?"

Here is my answer:
"No... it's already a steal. Just come and get it."

To which they usually respond by asking the address, and then typically rounding up the price and giving me the extra dollar just for the trouble.

They'll often do the same for you.

Now, allow me to wrap up this chapter by taking the pressure off you just a little further. I mentioned a few paragraphs ago that often sellers will start at an unrealistically high price, expecting to negotiate with their prospective buyers. In most cases, these sellers never plan to receive the price they initially put forward.

But what about you? After you've done a little research, made a determination about your probable buyer and your competition, and established what you believe in your heart to be a reasonable and fair price, it is still common for people to go against their best judgment and their best interests, and lower the price with the very first prospect that calls. Why?

I believe I found the answer.

In analyzing my own early sales on Craigslist, the reason that I felt the need to cave to the first buyer is because I really wasn't sure there would be a second buyer!

I had become so conditioned to the low expectations of the garage sale mentality that I actually believed this was likely my only chance to make the sale.

**I didn't understand (as I do today)
that there is almost always another buyer.**

Now, I should also tell you that my first ads on Craigslist were bad – really bad! You see, when I first started, I didn't have a guide like this one to quickly and effectively teach me the ropes. So I looked at other ads on Craigslist, modeled mine after those, and learned that most of them aren't selling anything!

Worse, by making my ads look like all the rest, there was nothing at all to make my ad stand out from the crowd – to call attention to the fact that I had something really special to sell. It was so disheartening to run ads and have absolutely no one call whatsoever...

...and then, one day, it happened.

I placed an ad that literally did everything wrong and yet, to my surprise, several hours later the phone rang! I answered, and I couldn't believe someone had actually responded to my ad... my heart was actually pounding!

The item that we were selling was a gorgeous culinary wood cutting block – a real work of art. Finely crafted of beautiful end grain northern maple, this stunning kitchen piece was brand new – never used – and had been purchased for just under $120.

> Not knowing what I was doing,
> I did what I saw others doing.

I slashed the price to nothing and figured I'd get even less. I believe the entire posting had 12 words. It had no pictures. It had no captivating headline. It had no story. This was it:

> "Wood cutting block $35 never used.
> Dimensions are 18" diameter, 3 1/2" height."

Now, I'll admit, with an ad like that, I had low expectations. Did you ever notice that you often get in life exactly what you expect?

The very first caller asked where we were located, said he was in the area, and had a $20 bill on him... would I accept it?

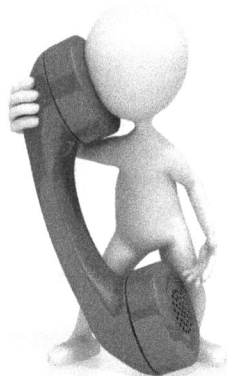

So what do you think I did?

Yup, you nailed it... I said sure, why not, come on over and get it. And why did I do that?

I was afraid that first caller would be the only caller.

Seven billion people on the planet...
nearly five hundred thousand of whom
live within a short drive from my house,
and "Bob" was going to be the only one!

As if I couldn't repost it again a few days
later with some different copy
and attract some different attention.

Are you ready for the rest of the story?

As bad as that ad was, within the next few hours I had three other potential buyers call, each willing to pay the full $35 I asked for in my ad.

Further...
had I known what I know today...
had I understood what I'm sharing with you now...
had I identified the value it had to the right buyer...

I'd have likely sold it for at least twice that.

Chapter Four

Know Your Competition

"There's no better friend to any merchant than a fair competitor."
– James Cash Penney

Here is the truth. You are posting your ads on Craigslist for one and only one reason:

You want to sell your stuff.

And as long as we're at it, let's look at another truth: there are other people out there who have the same or similar items, and they'd like to sell their stuff, too.

Imagine that.

And therein lies a concept that you want to become not only familiar with – but also comfortable with. For here is yet a third truth: competition makes us better.

So there it is... a seminar in a nutshell!

- ➢ You want to sell your stuff
- ➢ Other people want to sell their stuff
- ➢ This competitive situation makes us better

Generally speaking, it is also good for the customer!

Competition isn't just for the big firms on Wall Street or the professional sports teams. It is for you and me, and is something you have likely experienced.

If you've ever competed for a job or promotion – or the love of a parent or potential mate – you know what I'm talking about. And the same principles apply when looking to attract the attention of potential buyers for your merchandise on Craigslist.

Now, before you start to worry that you'll need to take a marketing course to make some quick web sales, let me put you at ease by making two statements:

1) It is really easy to separate yourself from your Craigslist competition, and
2) I will teach you everything that you need to know to succeed

Let's break this down:

Compared with traditional business – whether in big corporate America or the hardware store down the street – you have one very great advantage when entering the online sales and marketing world on Craigslist. *I can't stress this point enough!*

You see, it is quite likely that none of the advertisers that are competing with you for the attention of your potential buyers have any sales or marketing experience – none whatsoever!

Compare that to the small business person who is up against the big box stores and their huge budgets and professionally trained staff seven days a week. On the contrary, you are competing with Joe two blocks away or Sally across town. Chances are, they are busy... they are tired... and they are not professionally trained. I believe I know very well who will win that competition, and I am personally betting on you!

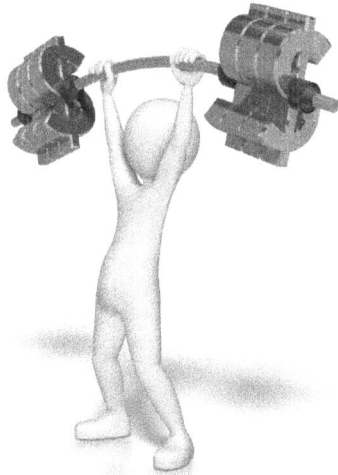

The reason is simple. You are right now investing in learning powerful and easy-to-apply strategies that have allowed me to sell thousands of dollars of personally-used merchandise on Craigslist, and develop relationships along the way with people who refer other buyers to me. Copy the actions, and I believe you will receive the same results.

Remember from chapter 3, we have two simple jobs:

1) First, create awareness
2) Second, create preference

**Don't make it any more difficult than that.
Let's look more closely at your competition.**

Mary is a stay at home mom, and Jim is a school teacher. Bob is a mechanic, and Julie works at an office. All have a few items to sell and low expectations of the process.

➢ They've put signs out in their front yard and tried to sell stuff before
➢ They've talked to friends, neighbors and relatives and felt pushy
➢ They've held garage sales and rummage sales and dread the process

Now, recently, they've heard about Craigslist, signed up for a free account, and written a few ads that look like just about every other ad posted on Craigslist. The results? They're not pretty:

➢ No phone calls
➢ No response
➢ No sales

This is your main competition on Craigslist, and you are going to quickly, easily, and effectively grab the awareness and preference advantage by applying the simple steps and guidelines outlined in the following pages.

As the old saying goes, knowledge is power. But the real truth is one step beyond that – it's the *application of knowledge* that has all the power.

Not only will you learn the techniques, but you will also begin to immediately apply them to the process of selling your items, large or small.

I believe you'll see the results as soon as you do.

As mentioned previously, you are competing with other Craigslist advertisers for the attention of your audience – *you want your buyer to notice you.*

You're also competing with other advertisers to win the preference battle in the mind of your audience – *you want your buyer to choose you.*

Now, please hear this:

Your buyers, like mine, have absolutely no shortage of choices. This realization guides all of our other activities in the process.

Not only can they buy from one of umpteen other Craigslist advertisers in your city, but they could also broaden their search (and their risk) by going to an online auction such as eBay or a market such as Amazon. They could search local thrift stores or shop at garage sales.

Then again, for the right price, they may consider buying brand new at any one of a number of retail stores, or... they may just decide to wait and do nothing at all.

What does all this have to do with you selling some unused clothes, furniture, exercise equipment, or household appliances on Craigslist?

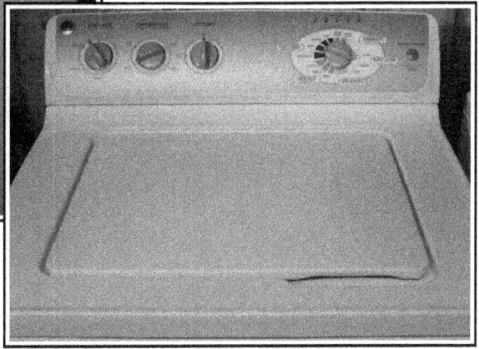

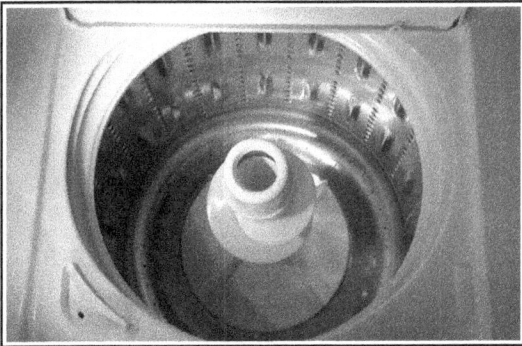

Well, just about everything! Your job is to use your creativity to attract their attention, and then get them to take action and purchase your item – today!

In the next chapter, you will learn the components of a winning ad and you'll create your first one. You'll be using information that you pull off the Internet about your competition to structure your pricing and to give the buyer a reason to buy from you.

Total time investment: 5-7 minutes.

And here's the really great part – almost certainly, those who are placing ads for similar or even identical products will not have done this.

That means that whatever you're selling, you have the advantage in getting the buyer's attention, and receiving preference in their decision process.

Simply stated:

Your buyer will WANT to buy from you!

Chapter Five

Writing Your Winning Craigslist Ad

"Many a small thing has been made large by the right kind of advertising."
– Mark Twain

Having spent my entire adult life in business – and marketing and sales in particular – I love that quote!

And it's the truth!

However, what Mark Twain never envisioned was a platform where you could do extensive advertising that could reach the whole world... for FREE!

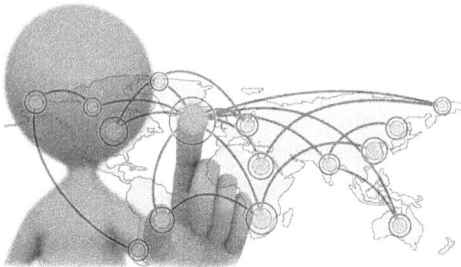

But that's what you have available today with Craigslist, and right now you are about to construct your first Craigslist ad that will really get the attention you deserve and give you the opportunity to hone your people skills and sell your stuff!

You've already taken a few minutes to:

- ➤ Learn the advantages of selling on Craigslist
- ➤ Study a bit about your competitors
- ➤ Identify your options in pricing
- ➤ Research your item's value
- ➤ Identify the benefits for your buyer
- ➤ Discover your story with your product
- ➤ Consider your process with callers

Now, let's pull it all together and create your winning ad!

Here are the nine components that you will include:

1) A powerful and attention-grabbing headline
2) Your general geographic location
3) Your story and your product's story, written with common search terms
4) The exact price for which you will sell
5) A summary of your sales process
6) A compelling call to action (do it now)
7) A statement thanking them for their interest
8) Your first name and contact info
9) Digital images

Look at how I used each of these in an ad that received enormous and immediate response!

The Best Snow Blower Of Your Life!
Location: By Airport

Moving this month to a new place that provides all maintenance so we won't be needing this awesome Arien's ST824 Snow Blower.

When we purchased this beauty brand-new, it retailed for $1549 and we paid $1429 on sale with the delivery charge.

I know there is someone who appreciates quality and wants to save seven or eight hundred dollars on an exceptional machine like this.

I'll tell you it's $625 and you can offer $100 less, or I can just tell you the bottom line price is $525... your choice. Either way you win, as the price will go up with the first big snow fall.

Your opportunity to own this will be determined by the order in which your call is received. Grab your cash, and come get your beautiful new machine.

Thanks for your interest,
Steve
(xxx) xxx-xxxx

I will go deeper into the strategies I use in my ads when we come to chapter 7.

In the meantime:

➤ Can you identify the individual components of the ad?

➤ How does this format compare with the ad for the heater back on page 41?

➤ Log onto Craigslist and look at just about any competing ad... whose ad would you call?

Also, as is par for the course, nearly every ad in the same category had serious and (in most cases) easily correctable flaws – corrections that could likely have brought an extra $100, $200, or more to each of these sellers.

But they didn't know.

Here they were, pricing their items hundreds of dollars lower than they needed to... and they still couldn't sell them against mine. By the way, when I placed my ad, the price was $175 more than the next closest offer... and it sold in less than 24 hours.

Pricing too low is one of the biggest mistakes made by Craigslist advertisers. I'll cover it and others in the bonus chapter. For now, check out a handful of the pics I used in the snow blower ad, and we'll expand our image strategy in chapter 7!

Ready to write your own ad?

Let's begin with your headline. Over time, you'll come up with a handful of your own that work well for nearly any ad, but let's start with a few of mine.

Take whatever item you are going to sell, and place it into one of the <blanks> below:

- ➢ *The best darn < > on Craigslist...*
- ➢ *The most beautiful < > on Craigslist...*
- ➢ *The most powerful < > on Craigslist...*
- ➢ *The quietest < > on Craigslist...*
- ➢ *You won't find a better < > on Craigslist...*
- ➢ *I wish I could keep this < > forever...*
- ➢ *You are going to love your new < >...*
- ➢ *The highest quality < > we've ever owned...*
- ➢ *I have your new < >...*
- ➢ *This is the < > she's been asking for...*

You get the picture.

"Your beautiful new refrigerator is here!"
beats
"Fridge in working condition. $100 obo"

...every time. Now you try it.

By the way, here is the ad that sold our refrigerator for $220 in less than six hours. NOTE: That was $31 more than I asked for in the ad.

The Best Refrigerator on Craigslist!
Location: By Airport

We're moving to a new place that is furnished with all kitchen appliances. Would absolutely LOVE to take this with us but they won't allow it.

That means someone's wife, mom, daughter, or girlfriend is going to be thrilled with her beautiful and ultra-clean new fridge! Heck, you might even buy it for yourself!

This is without a doubt the highest quality appliance we ever owned. It is awesome... Whirlpool 25 cubic foot, 32" deep with handles, 35 1/2" wide, and 68 1/2" tall... and it is priced to sell tonight at $189 cash. No negotiating – it is a steal.

Your opportunity to own this beautiful appliance is dependent on the order in which your call is received. It will be in your home by Monday or we'll take it with us and sell it at our new location.

Thank you for your interest,
Steve
xxx.xxx.xxxx

Here are just three of the eight images that I included with that exceptional ad:

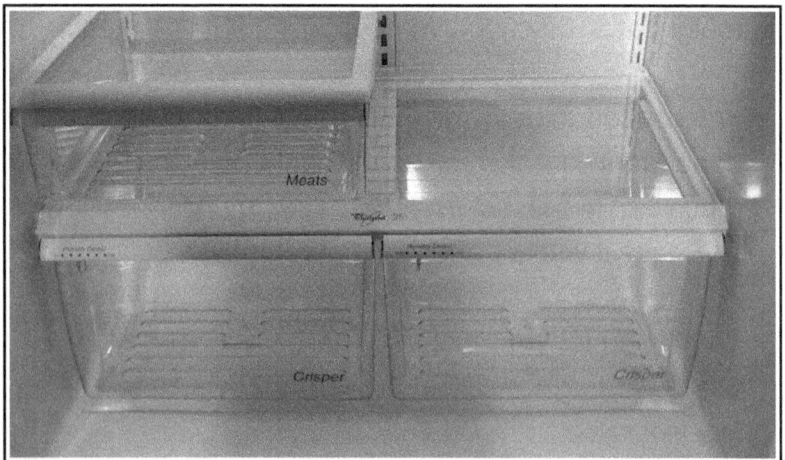

Next, when composing your ads on Craigslist, there are fields for price and location.

For strategic reasons, I leave the *price* field blank, and will share the reason for that in chapter 7 along with other strategies.

Right now, leaving it blank will simply save you about two seconds and it is one less thing to do! You'll include the selling price in the body of the ad.

You'll also notice in my postings that I use a very general location, like "By Airport," as opposed to using my home address or the map function that is available.

I see others who seem to be willing to put all their personal information out on the web, but I never do. For me, it is a simple matter of my desire to maintain a reasonable amount of privacy. In fact...

...the only person who will receive my home address is the one who is on their way over right now to purchase the item I am selling.

NOTE: *There is no reason to give personal information to strangers on the Internet who may not even be sincere or qualified buyers.*

So, skipping the price and adding in your general location took all of three or four seconds.

You are literally minutes from publishing your first ad that really gets attention on Craigslist!

**It's time to tell a few stories,
and then wrap it up.
Which stories?**

1) Your story – when and for how much did you originally buy the item and why are you selling
2) The item's story – what makes this product so special and what is the benefit to your buyer
3) The pricing and sales process story – what is the bottom line and how should the buyer respond
4) The action story – the compelling reason for them to get on the phone right now

Look through the actual ads that are reprinted on pages 41, 61, and 65.
You'll see similar stories told over and over.

More importantly, you'll see advertisements that get attention, create preference, and sell time and time again.

That's Quick Web Sales in action!

Then close it out.

➢ Thank them for their interest

➢ Provide your contact information (you'll be amazed how many people forget to do this)

➢ And continue on to add your images

Attention Grabbing Headline and Location

Your Story _____
_____
_____

The Items Story _____
_____
_____

The Selling Price _____
_____

The Sales Process _____
_____

Compelling Call to Action _____
_____

Thanks

Contact Information _____
_____

Images

Ready to set up your Craigslist account?
Follow these easy steps!

(a reprint of the process is included on page 131)

The account sign-up checklist below is the process as it stands as of the date of publication of this edition of *Quick Web Sales: A Beginner's Guide To Selling Your Stuff On Craigslist*.

Should Craigslist modify their account sign-up process, the changes will be reflected in future editions of this book.

1) Go to www.craigslist.org
2) Click on your city, or one near to you
3) At the top left, click "my account"
4) Click "Sign up for an account"
5) Enter your e-mail address and verification code
6) Click "create account"
7) *Follow the instructions to set up your password*

Chapter Six

Safety, Privacy, And Common Sense

"My greatest strength is common sense."
– Katharine Hepburn

I love selling on Craigslist, and soon you will, too.

In fact, if you're like many people, you didn't even wait to read this far and you've already put up a few ads and sold some stuff.

Congratulations!

You've also likely been both surprised and pleased at how streamlined and successful the process was after you implemented just a few of the nuggets in this beginner's guide.

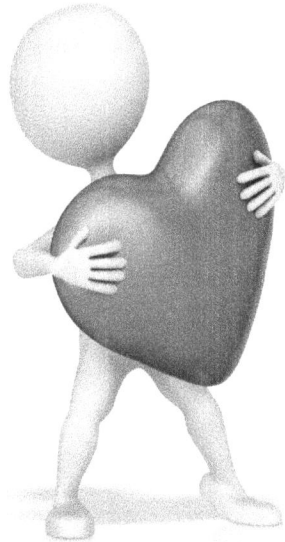

Now, please allow me to share just a few additional thoughts on selling in the online or Craigslist environment, as it relates to privacy and security.

Although today, I see the solution to everything described in this chapter as nothing more than common sense, when I was just getting started, it wasn't common – at least to me.

➢ I didn't know what I was doing

➢ I hadn't thought things through very well

➢ I just wanted to sell some items I wasn't using and get some additional cash to use for whatever I needed that week

I was also over-eager, and often gave out too much information to people that I didn't know or trust.

Further, I didn't realize that there are some really easy ways to weed out those who aren't serious, those who just waste your valuable free time, or those who might actually be part of criminal activity on Craigslist.

Criminals... on Craigslist?

Yup, happens every day... but it doesn't have to happen to you.

There are simple steps you can use to separate yourself from trouble, and from troublemakers.

The three main principles to keep in mind when selling on Craigslist are:

1) It is your property. You can choose when, if, and to whom you will sell your things
2) You can maintain a high degree of anonymity and separation in the sales process, and can shut it down at the first sign of something you don't like
3) It is always wise to trust your gut – your intuition

So, let's talk about privacy and financial safety.

For me, maintaining my privacy begins with the application of four simple rules:

1) I do not publish my full name
2) I do not publish my direct telephone number
3) I do not publish my home address
4) I do not use the map function that is offered

Though that wasn't always true.

In fact, I had to learn the hard way. Early on, I used my home phone number, which can often be easily tracked online to your physical home address. Later, after abandoning our land line, I published my direct mobile phone number – or worse, on one occasion, my wife's mobile phone number.

So now, here was my sweetie – busy with family members or engaged in the activity of her choice in her spare time – and suddenly she had to jump every time the phone rang.

That is not the way to go.

Instead, here is what I recommend:

Set up a free Google Voice number that you can use to receive messages, screen callers, and take control of the process. I'll share more with you about that in the next chapter.

Even better, get several of them and record a distinct message for each ad that you place and lay out the terms for your buyer. **There is an exact transcript of one of my voice messages for you on page 99.**

This does several things. Not only does it provide that level of separation that we spoke of on the previous page – it buys back your peace of mind and management of your time. Further, used properly it also tends to weed out the tire kickers and those who aren't willing to leave their personal information.

This is important.

People have been taken advantage of, and even robbed, by someone claiming to be so-and-so who just happened to call on a public phone using a false name. That doesn't happen when they must leave me a message and I call them back at my convenience.

Logically, safety concerns become more of an issue as the value of your items increase.

Here are just some of the higher-end items that we've listed and sold over the years:

- washers/dryers
- refrigerators/freezers
- golf clubs, dining sets
- sofas, loveseats
- rockers/gliders
- lawn mowers
- snow blowers
- garden equipment
- clothing
- electronics
- toys, jewelry
- art work, kitchen utensils
- light fixtures, heaters
- hand tools, power tools
- construction equipment
- tables, chairs
- decorative pieces
- and much more!

Here's a statement you can take to the bank:

**The higher the value of your item,
the more scammers you will attract!**

We once listed a gorgeous upright piano for $6200 – and oh, did that bring them out of the woodwork!

WARNING: Scammers will try to excite you, confuse you, and get your bank or PayPal account info. Don't fall for it – deal ONLY in CASH!

Here are actual e-mails (typos included) that I began receiving within 60 minutes of our listing going live:

On Jan 31 Ted C. wrote:

"Please confirm is piano still for sale?"

Reply from me:

"Hi Ted, Serious buyers only,... please call the number listed. Thank you."

Ted C. to me:

"Okay Am trying to know condition because am buying it for my brother, so can you assure me that i will not be disappointed, also no shipment involved as i have a mover that will come over for the pick up and am satisfied with your firm/advert price, as am requesting this transaction should be done via PayPal so the PayPal charges is on me and Payment will be made via PayPal only get back with your paypal email address."

****

Oh sure. All I have to do is send my PayPal account information to an anonymous guy named Ted, and he will deposit the funds at once! Yeah, right.

Here is a different but similar exchange:

On Jan 31, Michael S. wrote:

"What is the lowest you are willing to let it go?"

Reply from me:

"Hi Michael, The price of this beautiful instrument is $6200. Thank you."

Michael S. to me:

"I've read through the ad and I'm satisfied. I would have loved to give you call and discuss with you over the phone about the listing, but I'm currently out of town on a geophysical investigation in the mountains and won't be back in town until 25th of Feb. So coming to your residence for inspection won't be possible at this very moment but will appreciate it much better if you can get back to me with its present condition...

I would love to make an instant purchase, and will be paying through my PayPal account that is attached to my bank account. You will be notified by PayPal as soon as I make the payment in to your PayPal account, and you will be able to receive your money directly from your bank. You can set up your own account with PayPal if you do not have any. Simply log on to www.paypal.com and create your own account; it's free.

If you already have a PayPal account, please do get back to me with the following information so that I can proceed with the payment or later when you have you own PayPal account created so that I can proceed with the payment.

1. Your PayPal email address,
2. Full name,
3. Phone number
4. And the pickup address.

And as for the pickup, I will send a shipper to come and pick it up after you've received your money. Please do pull down the ad from the Craigslist so I can be assured that the deal is on."

****

I think you've already caught the common theme. Here are seven red flags for high-value sales. The buyer:

1) Loves your product
2) Loves your price
3) Is willing to buy sight unseen
4) Has available cash
5) Is strangely unavailable
6) Has a shipper arranged for pick-up
7) Needs your account info to transfer funds

Would you like one more? My pleasure:

On Jan 31, James M. wrote:

"Do you still have the piano for sale and what is the price?"

Reply from me:

"Thanks for your interest. The price is $6200."

James M. to me:

"Thanks for the prompt response. I am ready to buy it now but i am not in town at the moment as i am a marine engineer manager and due to the nature of my work, it hard to make a phone calls and visiting of website are restricted but i squeezed out time to check this advert and send you an email regarding it.

I really want it to be a surprise for my dad so i wont let him know anything about it until it gets delivered to him, i am sure he will be more than happy with it. I insisted on paypal because i don't have access to my bank account online as i don't have internet banking, but i can pay from my paypal account, as i have my bank a/c attached to it, i will need you to give me your paypal email address and the price so i can make the payment asap for it and please if you don't have paypal account yet, it is very easy to set up, go to http://www.paypal.com/ and get it set up, after you have set it up i will only need the e-mail address you use for registration with paypal so as to put the money through.

I have a pick up agent that will come and pick it after i have made the payment...

Email me back:

1. Paypal id   2. your cell number
3. the price   4. your home address

Reading these now, especially with the typos and grammar and such, it seems almost humorous – except for two important facts:

1) Scams like this actually produce results for the criminals who perpetrate them. If such tactics didn't work, they wouldn't be used

2) Often when people have decided to part with a high-value asset, it is to alleviate some degree of financial stress and pressure under which they currently find themselves. At those times, and under those circumstances, the anticipation of closing the sale can cloud one's judgment

I am reminded of an elderly gentleman who is a family friend who was receiving solicitations from a well-known sweepstakes company that also sells magazine subscriptions.

During a period of great financial stress, he was purchasing new subscriptions weekly, assured in his own mind that he was about to win $5,000 a week for life.

No amount of talking would convince him otherwise until the contest deadline had passed.

The PayPal scam is just the latest twist in the attempts to steal both the identities and banking information of unsuspecting good people – good people who are in need of some extra money and who are blinded momentarily by their stress.

The rule for selling on Craigslist is simple:

➢ Cash is king – no checks, no credit, no PayPal

Oh... and also,

➢ If it sounds too good to be true, it probably is
➢ If it sounds crazy, it definitely is

In all the transactions that I have completed on Craigslist, I have accepted:

➢ Zero credit or debit cards
➢ Zero PayPal payments
➢ One – and only one – personal check

The personal check was from someone with whom I had developed a relationship over a few weeks and who had purchased a number of other items from me when we were moving. Remember, until the cash is in your hand, the ownership of that item is yours.

Then there's the issue of privacy as it relates to personal safety.

At some point, if you are to transfer ownership of your property from yourself to the buyer, you are going to have to meet in person.

Depending on where you live, the time of day, and the proximity to other people, there is more or less risk. Several pages ago, I mentioned the benefit of trusting your gut – trusting your intuition. If something doesn't feel right, the safest bet is to cut it off, change the deal, or rearrange the arrangements.

One of the oldest rules of thumb is that there is safety in numbers. When you're meeting someone you don't know to engage in a transaction involving property and money, the most elementary thing you can do is to conduct that meeting publicly or in the presence of others. Have other family members present, or invite a friend. Don't meet alone.

**Further, when inviting people to my home,
I typically have the item waiting in the garage,
or on the driveway or front porch.**

I don't remember the last time I had someone come to *"look at something"* inside my house.

They are coming to buy.

If it is a sizable item, I make sure they're coming with a vehicle that is big enough to carry it.

And I always have backup buyers. If, after we've made an agreement by phone, someone comes and suddenly launches into negotiating, I call the next person on my list.

If you live in the middle of nowhere and the item you're selling fits into your car, you can arrange to meet in a more populated place. Go ahead and change the situation to meet away from your home.

Let's say the voice on the other end says,
"Well, this sounds good – where are you located?"

At that moment, you have several choices.
You can answer their question by
giving them your home address
(which you may not feel comfortable doing)...

…or you can answer it with your own question,
arranging to meet at a public place.

For example:

"I can meet you in town any day this week, which direction will you be coming from?"

Choose a well-known landmark, shopping center, or coffee-shop parking lot to make the switch – any place with plenty of people around.

Taking just a few precautions such as these in the sales process can lead to a safe, enjoyable, and profitable experience for you!

Chapter Seven

Simple Strategies That Sell

"Selling is simple, when people want to buy."
– Steve Buelow

LOOKING FOR MORE ANSWERS?

Well, the truth is that I believe you already know enough to do a pretty darn good job selling your stuff on Craigslist – I really do. The purpose of this chapter is to help you turn good into great!

There are a handful of little secrets that I've learned and applied over time that have turned my early disasters on Craigslist into outright successes.

What's the best day to run my ad?

Should I include the price in my headline?
Should I set the price using round numbers?

What should I say if...?
What SHOULDN'T I say??

How many pictures should I use?

The simple answers to each of these questions are waiting for you right around the corner.

So, what IS the best day to run your ad?

Of all the questions that don't get asked, this is one that really belongs at the top of your consideration.

You are running your ads on Craigslist because you want people to come and buy your stuff...

And that won't happen if they never see your ad!

The search results on Craigslist are shown in the order of the date they are posted, with the most recent ads at the top. That's where you want to be.

I mentioned previously that I believe most would-be buyers on Craigslist don't really enjoy the process of shopping on Craigslist.

The last thing most people want to do in their free time is call on scores of people they don't know (and don't trust) and arrange to drive all over town to look at second-hand stuff.

Here's what they'd REALLY like to do:

They'd like to get the process over with as quickly as possible, they'd like to feel as though they're getting a good deal and not getting ripped off, and they'd also like to deal with a person they believe has integrity – in other words, you.

And it all starts with them reading
your ad on Craigslist.

You want to create an ad that:
Stands out from the crowd
Stops them in their tracks
Makes them call you now!

From a timing standpoint, that means placing your ad as close to the time when they do their search as possible, so it's as close to the top as possible.

For example, if you post your ad on Sunday night (when you have time) but your potential buyer doesn't read it until Thursday night (when they have time), it could be pretty far down the list of search results.

So what time of the week has the most people searching for items to purchase on Craigslist?

Pretty simple really.

People purchase things when they have:

TIME

and

MONEY

I typically place my ads late in the afternoon on Thursdays, just as people are rolling in from work.

Here's why: in most areas of the country, the following two days – on Friday and Saturday – contain the 48 hours where most people – at least in America – have a little of each, time and money.

FRIDAY IS THE MOST COMMON PAYDAY. SATURDAY IS THE MOST COMMON FREE DAY.

So, if they get the money to make their purchases on Friday, and they have time to pick up their goods on Saturday, when do you think they're engaged in the mental preparation for that to happen?

BINGO!!!
They make their plans Thursday evening!!

Now, things may differ in various geographical areas or in other countries where Craigslist is open for business, but the principle remains the same.

Plan to place your ads when buyers are planning how they'll spend both their paycheck and their free time.

As stated a few pages ago, buyers on Craigslist just want to buy – it is very functional. And they don't search ads and make reams of calls Sunday through Wednesday when they know they can't afford to purchase the item until Friday or Saturday anyway!

Even if they found the perfect match for what they were looking for, there's no guarantee that the item would still be available come the weekend, and then they'd have to repeat the whole process again!

So, quick recap:
What's the best day and time to place your ads?
Thursday between 4 and 5pm gets my vote!
(And it seems to work really well...)

Should you include the price in the headline, and should you price using round numbers?

Here are my simple answers:

"No and... no!"

Now, if you've spent any time at all researching ads on Craigslist, you already know that nearly every single one of them would suggest otherwise.

However, keep in mind that most ads on Craigslist generate a very small response, if any...
...and are selling almost next to nothing!

That is definitely not the result you seek.

Ultimately, you have two goals.
You want to sell your stuff:

As quickly as possible
and
At the highest price possible.

Here is how it fits together – let's take the questions in the order presented above. First, about including the price in the headline. When setting up the ad, Craigslist offers the following fields on top:

Headline. Price. Location.

I use the *headline* field and the *location* field,
and leave the *price* field blank. I suggest
you do the same. The reason is simple:

A lot of thought and effort went into creating your post. You want your potential buyer to read the entire ad – not just the headline!

If we don't include the price, but have a highly unique and quality-driven headline, the reader has to stop and click on our ad. They really have no alternative.

Think of it this way:

The average reader will scroll through the headlines on Craigslist quickly, seeing the same or similar phrases over and over again. In fact, there are hundreds or even thousands of them... virtually ALL the same! Sheesh!

Other than your ad, the listings look like this:
Washer $120
Washing Machine $140
Wash Machine $100
Large Wash Machine $150
Clothes Washer $90

…and on and on and on for what seems like forever.

Suddenly this just leaps right off the page:

"Hands Down, the Best Washing Machine on Craigslist... Period."

We both know what happens next...
...they have to click on it!
If for no other reason than to get the price!

And when they click, they also get the pictures.
They get the humor.
They get the story.

And the dream of owning the best machine
available for only a few extra bucks.

Done deal...

So what about the price – what about using round numbers like everybody else?

Here's the situation:
If you do what everyone else does,
you get what everyone else gets...

...which is just next to nothing!

Remember my story of the beautiful gourmet cutting board back on page 49? What a great example of following conventional wisdom... and selling myself short!

The conventional wisdom says to the seller:
Cut to the chase... be brief.
Set the price artificially high.
Give 'em a nice round, even number.

And here's what the conventional wisdom says to the buyer:
It's not really worth that much...
Negotiate.
Negotiate.
Negotiate!

I have another idea.

I suggest following a different path than the masses, so that we can end up with a different result.

- ➤ A result called success
- ➤ A result called happiness
- ➤ A result that ends with both you and your buyer feeling like it was a fair, honest deal

Here are just a few examples of items we sold during a recent move, *and I'll let you in on a little secret:*

In each case,
we received more than we asked!

You'll notice that in several of those transactions, we got significantly more than we asked. And in each of them, I didn't request it, nor did I expect it. I simply (and cheerfully) helped load or unload their vehicle, and received an added bonus without ever saying a word. **I think you'd agree that is sweet!**

Item Sold	Advertised Price	Amount Received
Miter Saw/Stand	$79.00	$80.00
Mini Fridge	$39.00	$40.00
Folding Tables (3)	$87.00	$100.00
Washing Machine	$189.00	$200.00
Dryer	$49.00	$60.00
Refrigerator	$189.00	$220.00
Heater	$59.00	$60.00
Rocker	$39.00	$40.00
Kitchen Cart	$29.00	$30.00
Lawn Mower	$99.00	$110.00
Shop Lights	$39.00	$40.00
Dining Set	$329.00	$340.00

Here's what I've found:
It is your buyer that thinks in round numbers.

When they go to the bank, they don't withdraw $79 – they withdraw $80 or $100. For that reason, when they come to make their purchase, more often than not, **they don't have exact change.**

On the other hand, I always have their change right inside my doorway – not in my pocket – and can run in and grab it in a flash.

Here's a typical exchange: they hand me three $20 bills for an item that I am selling for $59.

Me: *"Terrific, I'll run in quick and grab your dollar."*
Them: *"That's okay... keep the change."*
Me: *"Are you sure? I can be back in a flash!"*
Them: *"Nah... this is great. Just keep it!"*

I NEVER GET TIRED OF THAT!
And after spending all these years being haggled to shreds at rummage and garage sales... you won't, either!

$19, $29, $59, $109, $289, $349
With the exception of some of my earliest sales, my price ends in 9... virtually every time.

What should you say, and what shouldn't you say?

Your Craigslist conversations really begin when a potential buyer picks up the phone and dials your number. At that point, they are sufficiently impressed with your ad and they're wondering about two things:

Is the item still available?
What is the price they have to pay?

As we spoke of in chapter 6, I have several FREE local numbers through Google Voice which allow me to screen all callers and receive a text or e-mail alert with a time stamp so I know who called and when. This is important to me since I return all calls at one time and in the order I received them.

Best of all, you don't have your personal home or mobile numbers out there on the web, and you can record messages that are specific to the ads that you placed.

You'll also find it sets the tone for the remainder of your interactions with a potential buyer. If you don't already have one, I'll give you the steps to set up your Google Voice account at the end of this section!

This is what a potential buyer hears when they call me for the first time:

"Hi, this is Steve! Thanks for your interest in the washer that I have on Craigslist... it's awesome. In fact, if they'd allow us to bring it with us to our new condo and sell the one that's there... I'd do it.

This is by far the quietest and best quality machine we've ever owned, and it's going to make you or whoever you're buying it for very happy.

I paid $429 for this baby on sale at Sears, and I'm selling it for $189. No negotiating necessary... you're already saving $240, so just come and get it and I'll help you load the truck.

I'm accepting calls on this through Saturday night, and then returning all messages in the order I received them, so if you'd like to own this, leave your name and number twice and I'll look forward to speaking with you. Again, my name is Steve... I hope you have a terrific day."

Look what just happened...

In 42 seconds, I just reinforced all
the important points of my online ad:

**The exceptional quality and value of the washer.
The terms under which I will sell the washer.**

They also know that there are going to be other callers and competition for the purchase of the washer. I'm not calling anyone back until I've given the ad a chance to reach as many people as possible over a several-day period of time.

And if they choose to leave their contact info, they have signed off on those terms.

And that makes the
follow-up call
a piece of cake.

Remember, selling is
simple, when
people want to buy.

My return call sounds like this:

Me: *Hello Rob, this is Steve Buelow. I understand you're interested in purchasing the GE washer I have on Craigslist...*

Rob: *Uh...* (that is the word most start with) *yeah... is it still available?*

Me: *Yes, I'm just sitting down to return all my calls and you're at the top of the list. What questions do you have?*

Rob: *Um...* (the other word they start with) *well, I guess does it work really well?*

Me: *Yes, like I mentioned in the ad, if it weren't for the fact that we're moving, I would absolutely be keeping it... best machine we ever had. What happened to yours?*

Rob: *It died on Wednesday, so we're really needing to do something quick...*

Me: *Do you have a truck?*

Rob: *Yes, I can get one.*

Me: *Alright, well you know the price is $189 cash... when do you want to come and get it?*

Simple.
Now, there are two common questions.
Here's the first:

Q: Can you hold it for me until...

A: Unfortunately, Rob, probably not. *I've got umpteen other calls to return yet this weekend, and I'm giving you first dibs 'cause you're at the top of the list. What's your situation?*

Now, at that point, Rob may come back with a very good reason. For example, he may say that he really wants it but can't get the truck until Monday, or maybe he's out of town or something, in which case I will use my judgment.

At times, I've had people put some money down, and in those cases, they have always come back to complete our agreement.

In that arrangement, I will return ALL of the other calls, having a conversation similar to this: *"Hi Mary, this is Steve Buelow... thanks for your interest in the GE washer I have on Craigslist. I wanted to acknowledge your call and let you know that another person who called first asked if he could purchase and pick it up on Monday. He sounded sincere, so I will respect that and see if he lives up to his end. I'll call you on Monday and let you know either way just so that you're not left wondering... it really is a beautiful machine."*

Here's the second most common question.
Yes, you still get it once in a while:

Q: You said, $189. Would you be willing to take...
A: No, I wouldn't. Whoever I sell it to is already saving $240... I'm just giving you first dibs 'cause you're at the top of the list. If you're looking for something cheap, there's lots of others out there.

Almost always, they come and get it. They knew that was the price when they left their contact info on my voicemail. It was in the ad – no negotiating – and it was in my greeting on the Google Voice number. And if they were just playing games, it didn't cost me more than about a minute, and I call the next person on the list.

The most important point is to expect
the questions and have your answers ready.

Keep track of the most common questions that seem to come up, and then formulate your response so that you'll have a ready answer when you need it.

I believe you'll find that there are only a handful of questions or objections that tend to come up over and over again.

**To get your FREE Google Voice
phone number today:**

First, go to google.com/voice
Sign In with your Gmail username and password, or
Sign Up if you do not already have a Gmail account
Then, you will choose a new phone number,
which will be attached to your account

Second, set up your Google Voice account:
Click the **Settings Icon** at the top right*
Go to the **Voicemail / Text** tab at the top of the page
Click the box to send a message to your e-mail
Enter the e-mail address to forward to

* Google may change the layouts or design from time
to time. As of the printing of this book, the settings icon
is at the top right and looks like this: ⚙ ▾

Third, record your voicemail message:
Call your new number
Enter the PIN that you used to set up the account
Record a greeting specific to your ad

Remember, you can register for several accounts by
using several different Gmail addresses. This will
give you multiple FREE voicemail numbers to which
you can assign specific ad greetings.

Are there any good rules of thumb for using images?

Absolutely – glad you asked!

Even among veteran sellers, seldom do I see these simple strategies used on Craigslist:

- ➢ *Clean the item well before photographing*
- ➢ *Repair what can be repaired completely*
- ➢ *Point out any nicks, damage, or wear*
- ➢ *Isolate the item that is being photographed*
- ➢ *Be sure that the environment is well lit*
- ➢ *Take seven pics from different angles*
- ➢ *Upload your best pic twice (beginning and end)*

All of these tips have one thing in common:

They cast your items in the best possible light so you can quickly and easily sell your stuff at the highest price!

Seems like simple common sense... but you are going to be amazed at how many people don't follow these basic strategies. And that's just fine, because they're your competitors!

First, clean it up!

Take a second look at these three pics that I shared earlier from my personal Craigslist postings:

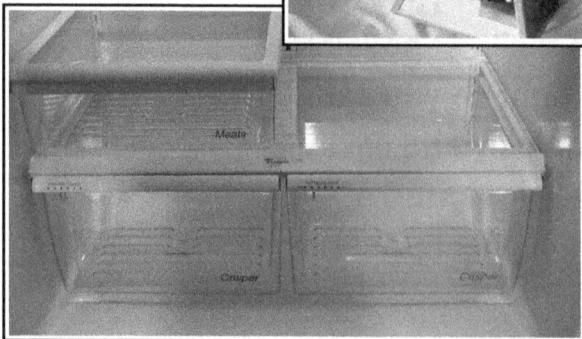

Because this book is in black and white, you can't see the stunning color of the snow blower and heater (which are both bright, blaze orange)... however, you can definitely see by the way the light reflects off them that they are clean as a whistle.

It took about six or seven minutes to wipe down each of these items with some all-purpose cleaner and transform them instantly into the best-looking items in their category. An older or significantly-used product may never look brand new again, but it can certainly look as though it was well maintained and cared for.

Next, repair items, if possible... but don't hide.

Along with cleaning it up, you may find that there are simple repairs or maintenance that could be performed to add additional value to your buyer.

For example:

When wiping down my snow blower, I found that a nut was missing from a bolt on the handle. Over time, it must have vibrated loose, and it could have been gone for years.

It cost all of 19 cents at the hardware store to replace it. Not bad, considering that I was selling this beauty for $525.

It is also common to find minor nicks and dings, or signs of normal wear and tear. From a standpoint of trust and integrity, I recommend highlighting these areas to your potential buyer. Turn back to page 106.

If you look closely at the snow blower pic,
you will see some light scratches along the
right side of the front housing.

Also, in the chute where the snow exits,
you can see a dark section where
the paint is worn off.

I could've taken the pic from a different angle
where this would not have been visible, but
that wouldn't have been the right thing to do.

The Golden Rule
– treat others as you'd like to be treated –

applies in all transactions and dealings with
people, including here on Craigslist.

Now, let's talk for a moment about staging your items for purchase. Staging refers to setting up the pictures to accomplish whatever objective you have in mind to accomplish. The good news is that you don't need to be a professional photographer to make it work for you!

Our goal is simple – highlight the best aspects of the items we're selling, and draw a contrast between them and all the stuff that others are trying to sell.

Here is the truth: it's really easy to do!

1) Isolate the items you're selling
2) Really light them up
3) Take seven decent photos

One of my favorite Craigslist stories is that of selling my lawn mower in the heart of a freezing Midwest winter.

I couldn't start it to show the quality.
The temps were below zero.
The gas lines were frozen.
The oil was thick as molasses!

And yet...

I had numerous calls within the first twenty-four hours, and it was gone within forty-eight – full price offer, plus a few extra dollars.

Each part of that ad worked – from the way it was written, to the search terms that were chosen, to the story that was told, to the care that was taken in cleaning it, to the pictures that were included, and...

...the sheer nonexistence of any decent competing ads whatsoever!

Oh, there were other ads for lawn mowers – plenty of them! Most had either no pictures or just one.

Due to Craigslist's copyright policies about other people's ads and images, I won't screen-cap them and print them here, *but I can tell you about them:*

Most were obviously quite dirty,
and had the pic taken in a dark garage
or shed somewhere amongst tons of
other lawn or garden equipment
and stuff piled up everywhere!

In one case, there was so much junk
I had to look hard to find the mower!

Fast forward to mine. I had taken five minutes to spray it down and clean it well.

I had also isolated it all by itself away from everything else, shined the brightest lights I had on it so that the light danced off the surface, and then taken seven pictures, calling attention to:

➤ Two different angles of the machine
➤ The manufacturer's logo
➤ The sticker with the horsepower of the engine
➤ The words *"Self-Propelled"* on the front end
➤ A close-up of the grass catcher bag
➤ A picture of the owner's manual

There was nothing even close... simply because no one else took the time to care enough to do it right. I suspect your market is not any different than mine, and you'll separate yourself from the crowd easily!

Okay, so why *SEVEN* pictures?

You're going to begin and end your ad with your most attractive picture. Image number one and image number eight will be the same – the first thing they see, and the last.

It's what I call "bookending."

The other six pictures will go in the middle, and it creates a very professional ad posting.

It's as simple as this: as of the publication of this book, Craigslist allows a maximum of eight pictures to be uploaded with your ad.

We fill eight image slots because it is the maximum allowed. If Craigslist suddenly changed their policy to allow five, we would fill five slots. If they allowed twenty, we'd fill twenty... you get the picture.

Imagine any business person refusing FREE full color print advertising...

...it's ridiculous, and it makes no sense at all.
However, that is what most sellers do on Craigslist.

Remember the awesome heater ad from page 39?
Here are the seven pictures that were used:

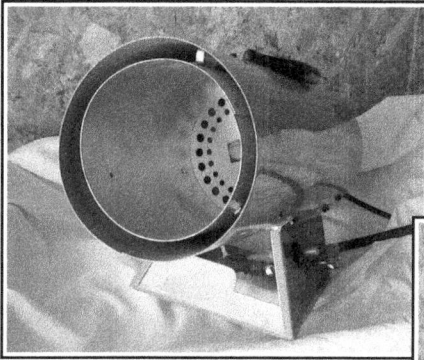

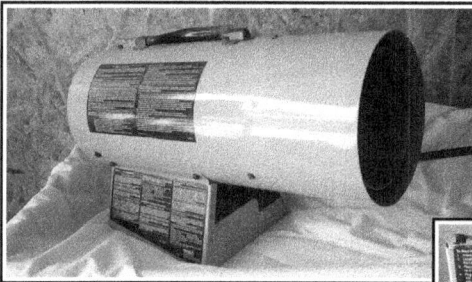

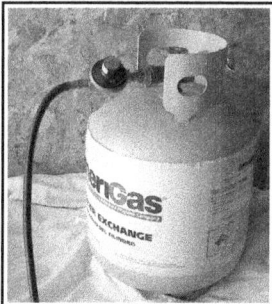

And here's the really terrific thing for you:

Rarely will your fellow advertisers (your competitors) take the time to do anything close to this.

In fact, you wouldn't know this, but I just stopped writing for twenty minutes, went onto Craigslist for my city, and then opened the first one hundred listings in appliances.

Next, I did the same thing for the tools category.

The combined total of those using their eight image slots was – you guessed it – zero.

Most had between one and three. A number of them didn't have any at all.

This is so simple.

Combined with the other simple strategies laid out previously for ad creation, you will stand out clearly, head and shoulders above the rest!

Avoiding The 10 Most Common And Costly Mistakes

Quick Reference Summary

Here is a summary of the most common mistakes that we've discussed throughout the book that frustrate Craigslist advertisers and keep their ads from getting the attention they deserve and their items from selling.

Under each mistake is a simple solution that you can apply in your next ad to improve the response rates that you are looking for.

Common Mistake #1:

Using a generic or boring "Product Descriptive" headline, such as:

"10 year old wash machine. $120."

Simple Solution:

Think in terms of the BENEFIT to whomever is going to purchase or use the item you're selling. The name of the product can be in the headline, but it doesn't need to be, because:

Craigslist has an excellent search function

And it will pull up all ads that contain the search term anywhere in the posting. It then lists those ads in date order.

Here is how I might write the headline for the very same washing machine, one with the search term "washer" in the headline... and one without:

"Without question, the very best washer you'll find on Craigslist!"

"Your wife or girlfriend is going to LOVE you for this!!!"

Either way, as long as the search term(s) are somewhere in the ad, Craigslist will pull it up. So I would work several of them into the posting, thinking about what others may search for... wash, washer, washing machine, laundry, etc. Then, whatever they search for, your ad shows up!

Regarding the length of the headline: as of the writing of this book, Craigslist allows a headline of 70 characters. There's no reason to skimp... remember, you'd pay for every line, or word, or character in traditional print advertising. Craigslist is FREE – use the resources to the limits that are offered!

Common Mistake #2:
Adding the price in the headline.

Simple Solution:
Leave it out. (It doesn't get any simpler than that!)

Remember, you want your potential buyer to read your entire ad. Give them a powerful and compelling headline and make them click on it to get the details. They are suddenly exposed to a posting unlike all of the rest, with your pics, your story, and your call to action!

Common Mistake #3:

Focusing only on the features of the
product in the body of the ad.

Remember at the end of the previous chapter when I
spoke about looking up a few hundred Craigslist ads
in the appliance and tool categories? At the time, I
was looking at their use (or non-use) of images, but
this 3rd common mistake stood out like a sore thumb!

In ad after ad after ad, the body was composed of
nothing but a short sentence or two, with a physical
description of the size or color, or stating the year
or age of the item. You'll find the same to be true,
with your competitors doing little to make their
potential buyers excited about owning the item.

Simple Solution:
Tell the product's story.

*It doesn't matter whether it's Craigslist or Costco...
people buy because of what the product can do for
them or how the product makes them feel.*

*Connect emotionally. Tell them when you bought the
product and why, how much you paid, and what a
savings your Craigslist buyer is going to receive.*

Reinforce the value and explain why you are now selling that item. ***And here's a secret:*** *every time you think of a feature, ask yourself what the associated benefit is for the person who purchases. Ask the question, "Why is that important," and write your answer into the ad. Finally, use humor if possible (it's always possible), and write like you're speaking to a friend.*

Common Mistake #4:

No telephone number or contact information.

Simple Solution:

Keep an eye out for the details.
It's amazing how many people forget to include the most important and basic information.

Before publishing your ad, ask yourself,
"What do I want the potential buyer to do next?"

If the answer is, "I want them to call me,"
then they're going to need a number to do that!

I close all my ads in a similar fashion, thanking the reader for their interest, and providing my first name and Google Voice number.

Common Mistake #5:
Attaching the words "or best offer"
(or the abbreviation, O.B.O.) to your price.

Simple Solution:
This is really easy – don't do it.
In other words... never, ever set yourself up to have to negotiate, or put yourself in a position to be nickel-and-dimed to death by every single caller!

Adding "or best offer" to your price says, "Excuse me, but I wasn't really serious about the price to begin with... just offer whatever."

In my experience, that is the quickest way to turn an otherwise fun and profitable process into one that is unnecessarily frustrating.

Common Mistake #6:
No call to action.

Simple Solution:

In sales, a call to action is one of any number of tactics designed to spur the reader to do something immediately. On a website, it could be a button they could click to receive a free product or report. In the body of your Craigslist ad, it is a reason to act now.

It could be as simple as one of these:

"How long do you think this beautiful rocker will last at this price? Come and get it!"

"I'll be returning calls in the exact order in which they are received. Serious buyers should call xxx.xxx.xxxx now for an opportunity to purchase this exceptional dining set."

Remember, it costs you nothing to add statements such as these to the end of your posting.

More importantly, they reaffirm the value of the product you're selling, while simultaneously placing a sense of urgency on the decision to take some kind of action at once.

Common Mistake #7:

No pictures, or limited use of pictures.

Simple Solution:

Follow the strategy laid out in chapter 7.

Create seven decent pictures from various angles, highlighting different attributes. Then, pick the most attractive one and use it at both the beginning and end, bookending the other six pics in the middle.

Common Mistake #8:

Using abbreviations that no one understands, or creates a puzzle for them to try to figure out. Imagine stumbling across this description:

**"15 yr old mach gd. Working cond.
Is bl & tund."**

Simple Solution:

*Just write it all out and give a clear picture.
As we referenced previously, you're not working with newspaper classifieds where you're charged by the number of lines, words or characters in the ad.*

In the example above, I think I get the first part... the 15 year old machine is in good working condition.

However, I have absolutely no idea what they were trying to say in the second line, and I doubt many others will figure it out, either! (If you do, please let me know!)

Common Mistake #9:
Setting prices in round, even numbers (like everyone else).

Simple Solution:
Find out what everyone else is doing and then do the opposite.

If you follow the crowd on Craigslist, you'll get what the crowd gets on Craigslist... which, most of the time, is not much.

Set your prices fairly, based on the relative quality of your items, and end the price in either a 9 or a 4, allowing the buyer to round up and give you the extra dollar.

I almost always use the 9, with one exception on very inexpensive items. If I don't believe an item is really worth $20 on the used market, I will price it down to $14, allowing the buyer to round it up to $15 if they choose.

And I have never listed a product for much less than that, choosing instead to simply give away or bundle small dollar value items as an added incentive or bonus to buy something else.

However, when you get into any higher dollar value items, for example, $29, $49, $89, $189, etc., I don't find any reason to negotiate or price down.

You've already laid out *the terms in your ad and your initial phone messages and conversations, and your buyer drove all the way over to your place, presumably to buy what you're selling.*

They're not likely to walk away over a few dollars, as they've likely spent more than that in gas if they turn around and go home without making the purchase.

Now... are you ready for the most common and costly mistake that almost ALL Craigslist sellers make?

Drumroll, please...

Common Mistake #10:

Not cultivating buyers to become
repeat customers or referral sources.

Simple Solution:

*Deal fairly, treat people with courtesy and
respect, and keep track of your contacts.*

Here are a few bullet points to consider:

➢ *Set prices fairly*

➢ *Return calls when you say you will*

➢ *Make appointments and be on time*

➢ *Uphold every agreement you make*

➢ *Under-promise and over-deliver*

➢ *Make a friend with your buyer*

➢ *Get their e-mail, Facebook, or social info*

➢ *Track your contacts*

➢ *Send a follow-up thank you*

➢ *Send a Christmas card or message*

➢ *Send an e-mail when you have other sales*

➢ *Ask for referrals*

➢ *Give them a business card or post-it note with
your personal contact information*

➢ *Throw in an inexpensive or unused "extra"
when someone purchases from you*

This last point can be a real winner.

I mentioned several pages ago that I almost always have things lying around that aren't worth nearly $20 resale on Craigslist, and the truth is, well... some aren't worth $5 or $10, either.

They're nice, but just not worth much on the secondary market, and they happen to be unused by me and cluttering up my space. It could be anything... a duplicate tool, or utensil, or craft item... anything! Just go through your junk drawers or basement or wherever this excess merchandise seems to collect in your home.

Then, give it away!

We often offer to "throw in" these types of items as a goodwill gesture of thanks, and most people really seem to appreciate it.

You may even do it with more expensive items that are just not likely to sell.

For example, we had several rolls of garden mesh that were in our garage for two years. When we moved, we no longer had use for them, and though *they were each worth $20 new, my wife gave them for free to someone who made a $100 purchase from us.*

The customer really appreciated it, and gave us his business card without us ever asking.

The Golden Rule
WINS AGAIN!

Now it's your turn, and avoiding these common mistakes is a sure way to make selling on Craigslist a more enjoyable and profitable experience!

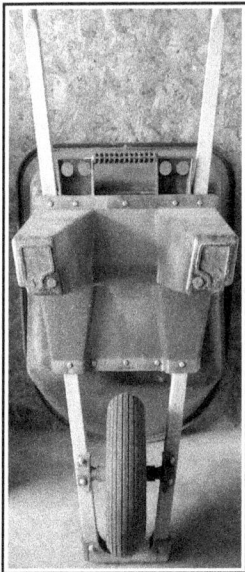

Ready to set up your
Craigslist account?

Follow these easy steps!
(reprinted from page 70)

The account sign-up checklist below is the process as it stands as of the date of publication of this edition of *Quick Web Sales: A Beginner's Guide To Selling Your Stuff On Craigslist.*

Should Craigslist modify their account sign-up process, the changes will be reflected in future editions of this book.

1) Go to www.craigslist.org
2) Click on your city, or one near to you
3) At the top left, click "my account"
4) Click "Sign up for an account"
5) Enter your e-mail address and verification code
6) Click "create account"
7) *Follow the instructions to set up your password*

As you've seen, getting cash fast and making quick web sales on Craigslist is easy once you know the rules...

...and once you have a system!

Are you ready?
You can get the cash you need today.

**We'd love to hear your success stories!
Visit us and share them at:**

QuickWebSales.com

www.ingramcontent.com/pod-product-compliance
Lightning Source LLC
Chambersburg PA
CBHW060612200326
41521CB00007B/752

* 9 7 8 0 6 1 5 8 1 1 3 0 7 *